OUR LAND IN THE BEAK OF VULTURES

Francis Annagu

First Printing, 2017

ISBN 978-1-326-93499-6

published by Hesterglock Press
The Blue Room
25 Wathen Road
Bristol
BS6 5BY
UK

www.hesterglockpress.wordpress.com

About the Author

Francis Annagu is an award winning poet and a Political Scientist. He writes in mind-blowing images, received the PIN Special Mention, PIN Most Awarded Poet 2016 and was shortlisted for the Erbacce Poetry Prize in England. He was featured on the Blog Talk Radio, nominated for the Nigerian Students Poetry Prize and a Poets In Nigeria Connect Centre Representative. His works have appeared in over twenty-five poetry publications, including Lunaris Review, London Grip Poetry Magazine, Kalahari Review, Crannog Magazine, Dead Snakes, Galway Review, Expound Magazine, Potomac Journal, Ayiba Magazine and elsewhere; also in poetry anthologies and blogs. Author of the poetry collection, Rain Upon Us (Classic Age Publishing, 2016).

contact Francis:

email: francisannagu@gmail.com
phone: +2347036161551

Acknowledgements:

Special gratitude to God for the inspiration to write this unequaled poetry book which has seen light at the tunnels end. It is with this I say thanks to Mr and Mrs Yohanna Annagu for their encouragement and prayers. I also want to thank SP Alex Annagu of the Nigerian Police Force, whom we're so proud of. To John Onogwu, Bayero Enoch, Bavoshia Asake and Mallambe Yakubu, I remain ever thankful. Lecturers of the Department of Political Science, Kaduna State University and the entire staff of the Faculty of Social and Management Sciences, I'm grateful for supporting me in this literary journey. Also, a vote of thanks to Paul Hawkins, co-editor of Hesterglock Press, it's nice working with you.

Francis Annagu 2017

Contents

A vote of thanks

The last time,
With red eyes we came for campaigns
Crowing in the near term,
Now with honourable intention we come
To harvest your votes
With a few Cowrie shells in the money-belt.
We have come to thank you on thick lips
For the selfless service to ballot and country,
Multipliers of luck and key-bearers of the city gates.
A carnival of post-election triumph
In procession like saints to our tables.
First, drink to forgetfulness.
Second, with sheer apology, we shall eat
From your pots of dreams and expectations rife,
Your's may be the sundown prayer
For more pots of soup, but alas . . .
We do not know too well the election promises,
We do not ever bother the Dambe* show.
Farewell to poor men stepping into darkness,
The windstorms cannot haunt the day
While greening trees straddle strong in the clay.
The voter's too weak to vote for life,
For the weak voters vote too soon for strife.

Dambe is a Hausa traditional fight

A priest at the motor park

At the motor park with his luggage,
Dabbling like a griot.
The clergyman saw some taxis queued,
Waiting to refill their tanks
While tax collectors probe them for licence receipts

Even as two diver's stooped under a lorry's exhaust
To check its smoke, trailing their head lamps,
As the winds pelt shop windows,
The inconstant legs of the priest en route
A ghost town in the night
Spread like clouds over the park's compound.

It came quickly to him,
That there is a brothel nearby,
Hurriedly down a narrow avenue
He walked up to rent keys of a trivial room,
Letting the prostitute's know his misfortune
Brought more coin more to their purses,
The turbulent time that shipwrecked
Him on their whisky circulatory desk.

National conversation

I will not ask the traitors of our land
Stories of the nationalists that stood
On the barb-wires of independence struggles,
They will not tell me how the nation survived.
I will not ask the rabid tribalists
That betrayed our course laid thousands of years
To protect the future generations against
The enemy's arrows, guns and boots,
They will not speak for the people.

I will not ask the corrupt politicians
How the nation progressed during economic misfortunes,
They will bury faces in the night,
It was them, the harbingers of underdevelopment
That loots our coffers, steals our cowry shells.

The flying football

It was in the grasses with grit we played,
With our rushing feet chasing the rolling ball
In the school yard as the setting sun
Dribbled between goal posts,
We knew the hourglass of life turned over
The empty tube for refilling our yesterdays
Cased in the game.

We played soccer of farewell with team mates
Occupied by future's expectations great,
Hopeful for more play-offs of friendship games
While we walk daily in holiday camps,
Like a league of goose
Pressing into lush mountains to write sonnets
For our coach, a clown with clave ,
With bubbles of love sprouting,
And watching the lineman points a shining trophy.
As champions, we were cheered by exultant fans
Below the harsh exposing clouds ever since,
The field grasses groan from our pounding boots.
The broken goal-nets dropped
When bewildered spectators scuttle
Into the referee's flute, an offside show
Unravels the final whistle of our flying football.

Mother
(For African mothers)

As we sit daily under the huge tree,
Canopy watching as mother flutters
In the scorching sun to the overgrown forest,
For the firewood of night warm.

When the cold shroud, our pale faces,
The scattered scarecrows of rattling snakes stand
On her pass through the broken stair-case of life,
Where lay the dry firewood of tropical trunks
That burn with engulfing flames and sharp glints of light.

As we watched the eagle glide clouds
To reach the golden towers with bridled wings,
The killing hurricane in wild whispers
Chases mother's footmarks through the shattered
Rafters of anthills; jeering whispers
trail to the gate post of her life,
While our tongues clutched mouth roofs
As pelting dusts plough our rapturous eyes,
Quarrelling with the cold,
Awaiting the warm firewood of life
And the boisterous sounds of mother's song.

Trophy

The time you won
The golden trophy we cheered you
Shoulder high from markets and towns,

Trying to fill the empty streets up with the news,
Possibly making sure
You have come home, athlete.

Poet on the run

At midday the poet searches
A key
Prettified with carats of gold.
Without a compass, the direction
East or west,
He tramps mapping with a pen,
The falcons' delightful swoop
Like spools of shadow patching
A river;
Ripple flowing on a bed of sands.

And as splashes drop,
The poet's papyrus ship sails
Onward, roving toward
The setting sun,
Where the key of muse he has found,
Glowing with cradle appeal and flint.

Beacon of echoes

Must we draw near the stream
That flows a direction unknown us?

Strong footed with bold shoulders
We shall walk toward
The beacon of echoes,
Where the eels flop out of torrents with profuse sweat,
Ready for scorn and swallow in daily show
While the coral snake dance fan-dango on the shores,

Hissing loud to the night's blanket
That envelops our cold feet, journeying
Through hawthorns and shattered shells,
Along the biting shores
Trees bend to let the rains
Pour and pelt us; quite drenched
Yet onward, smoothly onward we hold
Bonds triumphed with mouth strings in the echo.

The youths

Know you not that the youths are like
The nine-shooting stars rekindling the sky,
So dutiful to keep our country democratic
To nurture in peace, harmony and wealth
With pragmatic minds nourished, for a needful
Change to rebuild the road maps for sustainable
Development by day or starless night and search
For truth when the chicanery of lawmakers,
With a pressing touch
Of deceit beat the unsavoury drums of campaigns.

The youths are the offspring of tomorrow,
Overwhelmed with promising career and dreams,
The ones upon which societal comradeship lies;
Captains aboard a sailing boat,
Sailing on stepping stones to the golden ladder,
To be crowned and ever since, the historians proclaim stories
Of our youths strong footed on a long trek
To the conference room with fitted caps of wisdom:
This is to a millennium a tilak of hard work
And the key to break the iron bars
Of unemployment and crime and the thousand chains
Of extortionist regimes.

The youths are never silent to sectarian
Politicians with chants and echoes
Like ravenous vultures,
When misery and poverty spook;
Barred them from fellowship of country men
Mapping tomorrow's shaft of sunlight.

Quicksand of life

On the quicksand of life,
Some are sunk
Into sand-rooms
Of predicaments and derision,
While others, pressed down
Into murky waters
With tears
Under the scorching sun that burns.

Swallowed wealth

You succumb
To your world so fast
With not so much care for the lost.
Of dreams shattered, and carried
By the hurricane since
Expectations you wish to increase
Without fallow
do not follow
The scattered seed of tomorrow's planting
To bring you more harvest.
Yet your half-grain wealth was swallowed
By the vultures at night.

Elephant

As our nation remain climbing
Up on the plastic tree of wealth
For its penchant love for golden fruits,

We sit daily at the firewood, to design
Crumbling structures of its webbed-feet,
On slippery back of the banana tree-
A mockery to the elephant.
Plunking neck with over-greased palms
Up to the peak of the branch,

When our eyes has not seen
A mere haunt in midday, overwhelming
The tall slippery banana tree.

Yet strong pushing he keeps, as we noticed
Our vision engulfs for the end
Of the intriguing show;
But the mighty one in ravenous sound fell
On sharp, stubborn grasses.

Harvest of the sun

Dead seasons swiftly arrive upon farm houses.
Our misery a hand bell for the village clock
Hums in mournful sounds into goring miles
To the dancing hyenas in recital praises
Through the trees' rooftops, an indication
Of wild takings;
When the tropical sun swallowed the rains,
Ever since, the grasses have been silent,
The crops grunt in labour pains
Only to give birth to ravaging diseases
And killing droughts as our hungry
Children in the plagues cross
The dark riotous trunk-roads of life
Where death lives more potently, chasing
The forest fires to consume the ant's grain
And make us tilled out the ridges in vain;
A mocking season on its heels.

Protest

Strolling down a solitary pass in the embolden
Night, murmuring toward the gushing valley
To wash away blood of her menstrual stains
Under glittering stars of the nation;
A bestowal on the seeker, a kettle with the saint.

The wretched widow fell into sewerage,
Submitting to police boots
As night rains flush her through culverts
That break her national identity card in
The gulch of urine and rodents' dung.

While morning shows new teeth to sun,
The lizards scamper into cracked walls
On the brawling street, in troupe of heads
They protest to the government office to
*"Judge the widow her right or wrong or
Towers of whore houses will rubble down"*
As defiant men and mice plunder
Bazaars and barn, booty for their meal;
Over high denizen of corpses breeding,
The slum insurrections for justice shall prevail;
Read the placards: *"practice your gospel first"*.

But as the killings and looting went on,
Policemen eschew the situation,
That it was a tumultuous show to overthrow the regime.

Democracy

They are mouthpiece of the people
You vow, I rebuffed
The monotonous mutter,
I disavow
Their panel-beaten power;
You called a crown of honour
When the sun-tanning lizards crawled
Up into the cracked walls,
To take shelter in a dark crevice
As the shivering house tenants stand on the roadway
With bruised, blur faces the mayor you praise;
Flaunt their shoulders, shrugged
Toward the badminton march
As the rambling debacle brawls,
Leaving the house tenants bewildered
With languishing voices in the sunny week,
Filters into the dilapidated dam.

Road block

On rainy mornings
You will see them; drenched
On the streets, scavenging crumbs
From the wealth's trash-can,
On emaciated bones.

You will see them-
Peasants of this country,
Wandering along the railway tracks of anguish
Till the scorching sun burns
Their feet that walk over the roadblocks of midday.

A nation in a desert pot

Our nation potted in the scorched trough
Of a little desert pond, cracked in the ravaging sun.

A treasury full of gold and contracts but the poor has
No basket to harvest; fallow plots of niggard wheat,
While the wealthy over round tables seat
For cowries shell more in rowdy toasts to their iron greed.

Our famished nation drank a lot of wine
From vulture's pot of greed, ever since the thoroughbreds
Trooped the parliament gates, horrified a colony
Of those with deplete tongues and bellies
On a long trek to the house of coins and omelettes,
With urchins like killing predators
Tilling out store barns of ants in search of gathered grains
Under dark clouds of the nation's strayed bullets.

As the roofing sheets scorn thatch roofs,
The judge into the courtroom flutters
With a rogue wig for more
Justice miscarriage scarred on the faces of the poor;
As their blood rushes into weak bone marrows,
Like guinea fowls chasing the wind;
Derisive rains drop on their patched-houses.
The poor will remain hungry since their corn farm
Has no drizzle to grow seeds in the harmattan,
And when ruinous hurricane blows, death will make
A reap of the feeble people of ridicule.

Dancing tearful like the tropical trees reciting whippoorwill
Of mocking nocturnal birds, the shrilling cries heard,
As a sheriff passed by, amidst the corruption and oppression
Of rambling politicians carrying their trinket boxes.

Yet loud tantrums becloud the streets;
Labour union grouse with trumpets against inflated prices
Of petrol and food, when the giant politicians
Defied to throw water to our stunted nation,
The aggrieved in rampage trample police road blocks:
A cleared pass for the triumphed toward government lodges
And every step they take is toward the crack of dawn:
night has trailed thin anchor of the ship.

Boots along the hollering terrain,
Chants herald salvage to the politicians at noon's
Day heat, with low mouth echoes for food,
The chieftain's party behind heavy electric gates eschew
The turmoil of our nation.

Drums of triumph

We beat drums of new season,
For a corn dance through harmattan dusts tossing
In our visions and dreams
To boast of a thousand miles run on native feet
Trampling the thousand thistles so sharp that bloodied
Our bare soles to the merchandise's welcoming arms of gold
When the horrid nights with scarred face struggled with us
In the hills of discordant wailing and agony,
We persist with zest to reach
The wide field of dance and singing with high sounds
In the field beholden with gathered grains.

The search

It came to pass in the sweaty search
For our visions blown in shadow of snakes
With voices as thick as the night bird's thousand voices
Overwhelming our camels hooves travelling

Deserted roadways in swift gallop under clouds
That boasts of keeping the rains away from dropping
To wet our land wearing tassels of dead leaves
Through the narrow paths with sharp thistles
Piercing our sored soles like gardener's on a field of thorns

As we passed through trees with wild suspicion
Like the rattlesnakes combing rat holes at dawn
The ravens swoop the sky with mocking cries
Over our skulls with pelts of dusts and drench of the sun

Yet tired bones of our camels plough the road
As we drink from poverty's pot of hunger
Even as jelly fish dive out of dry wells

We search for corn and water,
For gold and nickels in barren mountains
And plateaus; where grasses faint and cannot grow,
We have come to pass in pursuit for fortune
And must take our hats off for the cause.

Town hall meeting

As pep-talk of the visiting politicians
Overwhelm the poor, they carry
Matters of the town hall meeting to probe
Cheap bones and brain of the masses,
Drenched behind doorposts with sun hats,
Even as their eyes never again set on rust
Teeth of the politicians, dressed
In fine-white brocades and denver boots;

The poor rested their bald-wanting
Heads on priestly shoulders of the vultures,
Thirsty but resting quietly as
Ravaging chicken pox
And deaths of malnutrition; children threaten the city.

A challenge, a task as thick as talons of the vultures,
Crumbling the wall of hopes
Into hot pots of poverty
Against bright dreams for tomorrow,

For the completion of tomorrow's Ivory Towers.
But worries bind with matters unsettled,
The tramplers ridiculing the trampled,
Envious of the rambling tramplers,

Change for direction turns
In favour of changers of time,
Historical, one eye taming the other;
The tamed with clipped tongues of pensioners
Protesting against policies of the tamers.

Looking down

From high above the magnificent sky,
I look down
Through the blooming trees,
To see hills and coastal plains
Sitting on the sands,

Giving home to roaches and the beetles,
While the wheezing breeze blows
Toward the praying mantis
Jumping bough to bough
In pure delight of the mangroves'
Evergreen leaves, azure.

From high above the palm tree
I watched as the chirping sparrows
Pick up scattered corns in the season of harvest,
Under the moisturising canopy of crepuscular clouds,
Even as the fog,
Upon the fallow grasses
Settles on flowing canyons.

Hand shake

The Ganges flowed into
The mouth of a tunnel, through a

Field where sprouting cocoyam
Grow to the sun, rushing

Through a strait along
A curator's footpath between

Trees, rocks and perimeter hills
As the sun retrench,

Hands shake of two friends
At the narrow bend
Tour the curator's pass.

For so long a time

For so long a time through
The road of our nation's bleeding heart we trek
In enthralled shadow of bulldogs,
All in tribute of freedom calling
From strange cries of amputated children
Ravaged with kwashiorkor to clenched beaks
Of puffins swooping brook to brook to drink.

For so long a time in becloud distance
Beyond tossing sand-motes of the harmattan,
We travel in tattered garments and shoes
To be crowned with painful thorns.

For so long a time in haste
Through the piercing brambles to unbind
Strong shackles of prejudice,
Before night rains overflow
Our smile carried amorously on the yolk
Of a tired donkey from Soweto.

For so long a time to break silence,
An entrance gate guard with arrows
Challenge us,
Yet in a rage arrive in servile chains
At the soap-box of a country
With weak teeth to chew our cheap
Dreams for so long we have tired.

On the navel

I feel a corrosive throb
On my navel
Moving; still, fast
Passes with plumule sounds:
Echoes and splashes.

It comes hurrying,
Tossing up
Things that munch
With cramp, my bones and flesh.
Ah, it was encased, the throb
Pressed in coal in my arteries.

I feel,
But no window shall
Let it out
For it chases away sorrows
So that
With gentle plush and fickle of rains
Shall I grow long as grasses
To feel the touch of the sun.

This country...

This country sprouts like a carrot
Among the busted thorns,
Fluttering out in the sharp blades
To the cruel sun.

With a servile smile that crumbles
In our dark bones:
A cocoon
Of deplorable roads and houses
And dilapidated motor parks
Shrieking loud
As we sit sedately on piercing
Nails, pricks and shattered glasses-
A combat to our bleeding throat.

To show the greedy parliamentarians
Who spread hardships
Over us, tormenting us under raindrops
Of anguish.
The profuse drops of rain overflowed
Our votes, chants and contracts.

A carnival under the sun

When the ants march with bags full
Of grain to the threshing floor
With a dance, the solitary glide of a desperate
Hawk show its turn to plunder;
The season as booty for its store barn.

When from the tractor plough on the arable land
We found the nuts of success and plenty,
The harvesters marvel at our future planted in sands
For tomorrow's cloud, rain and sun.

But when with our mouths we chant songs of elections
Here and there, like an army of locusts racing
With the armoured tanks,
The last of times will lay
Ambush with talons to crawl in our blur faces.

Electric fence

Our nation
Sit on the spiked seat of pain,
Each time with different voices
We hear him
Scream on the electric fence,
Bleeding profusely
As he watches a small fish
Dope out of ponds of anguish;
Innumerable, in a riotous dive
Signalling of injustice and cruelty,
While the police park
At the gambling house,
Carouse in feast with music and dance.

Predator

The city on our eyes;
Crumble down
With ravenous sound,
When a barn owl
Saw the tax collector building his buttocks
On the wheelchair of corruption.

Town crier

When the day's in mild glow show us
Bald-rump of the peacock as
Launching winds blow, we look
At the town crier announcing news of the earlier,
Meshed in sorrel-mouth of measles and malaria
As his talking gong wallow in gloomy sounds.

When the bones of our strength break on
Foundations ravaged by termites
That feasted into germinating seeds, mapping
Through green contours of our nation's progress,
The brutal tormentors crippled our ankles and
At night, as our languishing voices
Sing,
Never shall we turn away and run.

Corn dance

We trekked to the corn thresh-field
With dreams of a thousand grains
And the bud of a seed of a wheat of a thousand years,
All for a barnful of harvest.
A trek to the lawn,
A bestowal on the grain harvesters
With a new dance in the sultry sun.

A step into the world or wall

So dark our world,
When you open a book,
Find no letter in the scroll
But bulb-roots of scorn
And samples of war sprouting
From its spine to the scorching sun.

So dark...
The midwives delivered a child,
As strange birds perched
On the deck of the labour room.

So dark our world.
Show us the portion of life
With canopy wings of an eagle
Ready to shield
When the sky is cloudy;
Yet no rain crackled,
No earth smell of vegetation
But graveyards of plastic children
Ravaged with polio and malnutrition,
Scampering as lizards do
Into cracked walls.

Ghetto child

He stumbles on pot-holes and pot-lucks
Yet walks steadily,
Keeps it along the narrow road of life
That others tried and failed;
Child of irony in a world
Where the poor remain sharpening his knife
For a piece of bread, before the floods
Ride his dreams, his littles,
Fragments of broken pots and hope.
He remain searching, even without a find,
The ghetto child of conquest.

Shining coins

On the journey to the coasts of a world
Of friends with hooting owls in chorus
With the tidal waves,

While the sun has turned its face away,
The glow of the moon bright
Corn farm of the helmsman,

A walk out of town across
Sidelines of long plateaus
To harvest friendship forgotten,

From years past when tropical winds
Blew vibrant friends for life
Wanting more smooth

Handshakes of times shall keep a shining
Star in their faces
And early though the caller-birds swoop

Tree to tree to snatch greater moments
Companionship brings would have
No roasted corn on the barbecue,
When golden foot prints into golden sands.

Hold in nourishing times
While the eagle's wings, a huge canopy
Over the cleaving brothers, keep a
Cooling shade under the sun's scorching.

Fight at the newspapers stand

The fight left specks of blood
At the newspaper stand;
A heavy debt
To the drunk police chief.

Eyewitnesses led a mob; turbaned
With shawl and sheets, mumbling
Toward the edge, an enticing
Show along a garage of area boys
Sitting on travails of poor living

Who found a refugee licking
His stew pot, hit him to the ground?
The streets rowdy with another pain,
The grumbling mob chants
As their homes and farm houses
Destroyed by the new police chief.

Song of tomorrow

Song of the caller-bird strikes
The mountain crest;echoes,
Where lay painfully the great task
Of our nation,
Letting us know that a new
Rising sun and shape of the retarded
Plants would shoot
To the height of sky,
In burst of ever more spreading
To the market places and post offices,
To beautify in tinsels of beauty
The runways of piloted camels and abandoned
Classrooms, even as our tired shoulders
Carry yolk of the turbulent time,
Trekking long distances on bare foot;
We await the prophetic term.

Dead bones in the sea

Where the humming breeze run,
Bending through the bursting
Banana trees; there, swarms
Of hawks and gulls bury
Weak bones of the dead one,
Like madmen sowing the winds.

Because the sea has drowned
A poor fisherman helmeted with
A warrior crown to chase
The fish in labour pains, in a wild
Show of enchanting danger;
Danger to the night-returner
To his home, but never returned,
Even by the rushing chords of the flautists
Ever since, the voices of the praise singers
Have been singing to his dead bones.

A time in the reeds

Time has dropped in the reeds too quickly
With the lambent sun like a lone shooting star.
It was like a moment's peer,
When we use to sit daily under the giant
Iroko tree to welcome returning hunters from
The overgrown forest,
Where there is danger and turbulence.

So let no one steal from our pots of honey,
This land is for the brave ones.
Let no one come like the invaders to shatter our huge
Thatch roofs and crumble bamboo walls,
Letting the enemies trample our farms on mountain tops.
Let no one say to us song of the weak footed
As we pluck out night from its hiding shells
To becloud visions of the bats.

Our land in the beak of vultures

Our land has been invaded by the
Sojourning vultures
That come lately in the night quiet.
The males, the ones with bald-necks
That carried their young on their backs
Came with baskets and hoes.

The females, the long-beaked ones that
Tilled out our crops from the wheat
Farms shout in alarming sounds to
The rest; waiting for the harvest to eat
From our grains
Scattered on the rooftops
Of our homes resting on baobab woods;
The canopy of our home.

We are made people of the night,
The offspring of predicaments and plight,
Carried by the talons of mere birds
To a sky of ravaging dust
Under dark clouds that engulf our visions

But the sun is in subconscious sleep
As we clutch torches on our tired shoulders,
Searching another home found laying fallow.

Unlike us

Unlike us,
Our Creator is gracious,
Faithful and merciful
To the tearful and poor.

Unlike us, the greedy,
His heart a warm valley
Flows unseasonal for the thirsty to drink.

Triumph for our nation

With drums and dancing we announce
The triumph of our nation on the battlefield,
No more discordant voices
Across the harmattan thousand voices,
No more war zone and armoured tanks
But banners of peace
Flying beyond the hunter's trap.

We have murmured in unharnessed
Cotton fields, attacked with arrows and stones;
Ah, so dutiful, our triumphant nation now
Keeps a trifle count of shimmering stars in our eyes.

Sundown in the battlefield

Where from this stranglehold
Should we run
With our boots full of grouse
On the battlefield;
Our prayer wheels
We must wear to sleep
Under the night of terror and taunt
That portends the innocent child
With cries in the battle-fronts,
We must go with trumpets you warn
To the cemetery, a colony of those with olympian
Medals for a thanksgiving, not mourning
But only the torchbearers beyond us
Saw the horror, the slaughter slabs and hangman's rope.
Pray our journey is at the moon's horizon
When combing snakes play in the rocks.

Night rain on Southern Kaduna

Night rain fell on the tattered roofs
Of Southern Kaduna and many years
Will remain pockmarks of the invaders'
Knives, bullets and terror
While the profuse rains are turbulent,
Danger to the innocent mothers and children
Killed in ambush by ragtag herdsmen-
The plunderers, enemies of the peacemakers
Came like vultures, the harbingers of injustice,
Harbingers, harbingers spurning our call for security
Even while the twisted necks and bones
Of the aged and young
Littered the farms and streets.
But with supplications and watch the storms
Will calm when the liberators stand for the weak.

The parliament builders are gypsies

The gypsies to build the city's parliament
Arrive at the bus station,
But frightful of the town's silence,
Only bulldogs patrol the streets
Like some drunken policemen.

Builders of loot houses they are
Drenched in killing heat of the sun,
Builders of lodges of politicians and contractors,
They come in putrid clothes; ragged, tagged
To construct house of the ruling few
But to carry their responsibilities they cannot.

In tribute

Our land;
Standing between us and barbed wires,
Babes cry, humiliation,
Corrosive markets and plundered
Rice farms,
Grieves more ploughing the plain
With more dusts and drought
Although the victims are full of silent sighs
From the butcher's shop to fallen rafters;
The rain has refused to fall and dry winds
Blow their dream at dawn
While we wait in the court room
Of broken promises
For the exchange of thirst and hunger,
All in tribute of a cloudy day.

The harvest winds of life

It was winter,
When the harvest winds carried us
From the cowpea fields
To different directions of life,
To begin a new walk in the horizon.

The first harvest was a stranglehold
And the rodent's in your farm for a feast,
For you were too weak to plead,
Know you well the alarm.

The second harvest wound me
Into the sun,
As beaks of vultures mock
With a screech and I feared the ambush
On their old highway of greed
And for good the directions never
Conquer, but carried us to the barnyard of more grain.

The winning boat

Know you not that it is a bright sunny week,
A midday with clouds and glittering
Stars, for in expectations and dreams
On life's rough waters sailing,
The papyrus boat churns
Through a rocky strait that challenge our reach
To the Ivory Towers.
But sail shall we with smooth paddle
Toward the rising east sun;
In strength of a matador's spirit, life is strapped to a win.

Endless talk

The newspaper's report:
African leaders corrupt,
Roadside hawkers,
Classrooms abandoned and acrid,

While the radio houses chivalrously
Play discordant songs
Of war and military coups.

The clouds became truculent
With the situation;-
A story on the headlines.

Coffee house

The gentle breeze of morning
Carries sparkles of the sun

As the highlands glitters
With resplendent glow in the warm air

That petrol the grasses, weeds and shrubs
Growing in canyons of cold chilly nights

While the autumn leaves fall
On a coffee house sitting at the bend

The sounds of petrels
Shoot through the windows and woods.

Taxi driver

The taxi man
Left the garage quickly,
Drove into the rutted highway
Quenching its thirst
Under the raining dark clouds.
Street lights dim as a dinner Chinese
Lamp, road narrow with quills.
An old man and boy stood by the edge,
Stopped his aged cab.
He pulled over promptly.
While they ride
Into the chilly countryside,
Through hills, lakes and ginkgo trees,
They squeezed out a conversation
About Europe and Africa.

He won't let you down

Give your sharp ears to the Lord,
Lend Him your time
As your lamp you pass to Him
To refill the burnt-out oil of life,
He won't let you down.

When the sun burns the leaves
And the sandstorm tosses dusts so that
The Weaverbird cannot fly tree to tree,
To the Lord it must bow
From high above the sky,
So give to the Lord your cold ears
As you walk the pedestrian road of life
Where are shattered shells and bones and nails,
He won't let you down.

#0228 - 100417 - C0 - 210/148/3 - PB - DID1811419